Salamander Morning
poems

Salamander Morning

Nadine Hitchiner

QUERENCIA

Querencia Press – Chicago IL

QUERENCIA PRESS

© Copyright 2025
Nadine Hitchiner
Cover Art: Nadine Hitchiner

All Rights Reserved

ISBN 978 1 963943 46 7

www.querenciapress.com

First Published in 2025

Querencia Press, LLC
Chicago IL

Printed & Bound in the United States of America

I want
to tell you,
you are beautiful,
by turning thirty
in your arms.

contents

Moss Study
to R.

What a long rally. It is November in the evening, and the wick is short. But given the maple, and given the hornets—the pizzazz in the flurry—the phone will ring soon; they'll have a bed. And I'll not have a thing left to die in it.

It is only June, when there are two boys throwing sitters over the rain barrel. Their palms sink like lids, and even from afar, I feel a bulk to the balls of my cheeks. No one has a brailer to pick these cherries out of the waters before they furrow. In a bay, near Los Alcázares, I skip these stones

I have stood on, into the curls of the ocean. Into the shock of water that I had combed as rain back home, and that had left its gills on my coat. My husband worries about the distance—a mile can fill and fill, and my opinion's such an inadequate element—carnivorous and unattainable: near the shore, there is a rock formation that looks almost like a bear. I throw back its cubs. I fear what will happen if I raise them. My husband watches, and in the wind, I leave a hair in his laughter—

a ferry that we arrive on, in Dover, come July. We drive into the New Forest, day into a month. U–turn shortly after we see the horses by the river, a gravel lay–by into the green and park our car there like a white pebble. We walk along two bodies of water that are dissimilar only in their posture. Only by their ears. On the pond: pink lilies, white lilies—heads: neonate and flushed, then infant. I'd better my heart even for two ears, but I require confidence in their plastic. The river rushes along and we move through green algae, along the Havel on a small houseboat. Leaving Southampton, leaving myself behind; all that breathing like a grocery bag in the Solent, and no brailer, again. I steer, while my husband looks to change his glasses in the hurried dusk. Later, he points the boat into the wind and lets the anchors down, one by one. I switch on the white light on top of the roof. My left foot is out of bed by four, the other at seven the next morning. I pee out back and make coffee on the camping stove. The digger is still anchored on the hilltop by the lakeside—I cut the yellow

tulips from my mother's garden. The hydrangeas and roses, as well, to bring them into my own. I say to my husband: "I'm still here, after all", and so, I hang the balloons, wipe the benches and the tables. On my thirtieth, I call the magpies in, letting the Lametta sing in the wind beneath the canopy. I am not writing this without tears. I might have dreamt a little of death. Called the magpies in to take what they could carry—

mother bleaches my hair, blending what has aged with what hasn't, yet, like I am able to, on countable days. Asks, "should I come over and help with the dishes?" I must keep asking myself: "what is salvation worth, if I'm not here to feel it?"

Basin–Cut

With lines from "Here Comes the Sun" and "Yesterday" from the
Beatles, & with lines from "Hallelujah" by Leonard Cohen

to R.

Was there any room
for salt?
For one more pillar
to look back?

For the flamingoes to pink–en
in Torrevieja's lake—still, I did not see

the miles in the stone.

it looks as though they're here to stay

No, not that September, nor this May

on my thirtieth, so close to yours.

I was already architecture,
before Cartagena, only then
it was more clear;

I stood—still
blue tinted
window frames like veins on my breast
and my husband's shoulder
resting below,

kneeled
into my name, as if to find me.

here comes the sun—

I stood
over the basin back
home and picked threads
through the highlight cap—

dyed my hair
a colour close
to red.

Stood west of everything,
setting over its canopies.

Who is the morning? Body Language?

A bust—
a cut hill, salamander, salamander morning.

And

don't we yell,

      don't we yell.

I am not coming, nor am I going

from head– to heart–born joy—

what a house of scattered mirrors—
an envelope I have been too scared to lick—

If I'm afraid in it

I'll say "wind", when I mean to say "touch,"

If I cannot afford them a closed body,
what have I done, but put grief
into joy's chariot?—why only does that feel more true;

to have it chauffeur my sadness.

And

She tied you to a kitchen chair
She broke your throne, and she cut your hair

Since September, I've been skipping

timelines—find her by the fire, in clean clothes

and a basin–cut,

sleeping into me, already an afternoon.

And

here comes the sun

If I, too, bring a knife to the bow
of this timeline, it is out of habit—

for years I've neglected her, so

it is only to trim her hair—O Samson's
daughters—we shave each other's heads,

yesterday strong, and watch it grow back
wholly different.

I want to tell you what's on my mind:

I once visited Seattle when it wasn't raining
and I left

when it began.

Serif Serif

How is the room
between the cities
in which you live,
is there sleet—have you been bi again
?
I haven't had time
to find the right moment,
but I figure the dirt–
blue couch is only an hour long,
and the owlhead
of your shadow
contorts within it.
I have cored
my pear–y
hands, to give
you my sympathy—
how are
you, but that
?
You look hot
in these flares, is it
because you're manic
? Tell me about touch—
serif, serif,
untilunreadable.
Tell me
how a robin sat
on the mirror
cabinet in the cellar,
last year after August,

in an effort to be
unremarkable.
Show me this photo
of you, in your wedding dress,
that September.

Brushing through George's Hair by the Lakeside

A radio,

or for his hair to grow

down the mantle–

shore. I'd stand with my garden

hose and rinse the grave

off: in the coatroom, the lakesides would

do what they usually don't—

This going

crane, I think—would I move

where all the widows move?

June rain's hung out to dry.

I forgive

myself the ladder

I am building on

his eartop. For thinking of

him as sheet–

less like jazz. As a sidewalk

and me, hipless like a ball—

a dark, eliminating other darks;

I worry

my grief might fall

like a curfew

to life. We talk about Jennifer

and autism. Her son, on the swing

sets with it and Tourette's.

I see myself there,

too, with something

I could be mistaken for.

To George, in the Distance

When I hold you
with my left eye,
I forget
the colour of hornets,
through the panel
of their wings. I want
to tell you,
you are beautiful,
by turning thirty
in your arms.
Wednesday, I cried,
was honest as a bottle—
glogg–glogg–glugged before
I even said a thing.
I'm walking through the market,
though your room of ashtrays
full of goldfish,
its basin cut shadow, airy
behind the light.
Despite the weather, we
bark like a stray
cloud meeting another,
with nothing
but a strange scent
to offer each other.
Through to the stall with the raisin
necklaces, hanging from the canopy,
and find in one that ladybug
with six dots, that you saw on Tuesday,
ogle at it
like at the monument
in Cartagena, on Wednesday.

I snorkel on, through this rain,
to the car in which you take me
down the long coast road
and the swampy field,
to the pharmacy
to spend a 10'er.
More and more of your father practices
itself on you. In your voice, the ferry
from Calais to Dover.
The sun is sedated
by our speed, and its light,
lightning. Swallows swim low, through
the raisin, pick insects
from the sky. Everything is
moveable, even us.

The Ungiving

After your father texted, "the pigeons have hatched!"

I felt the gift of life,
and the immediate counterpart of it

merge across the English Channel,
felt it even in the threads

of my nightgown, pulling
the silk back into the worm that spewed it,

and I stood in the bedroom, naked
of death. Ungiven it.

In your father's garden, everything
is life, which sometimes means "memory"—

the pebbles, the rose
from your Nan's Garden.

The frogspawn growing their chirps,
and the goldfish spawning—between them

the small pathway, the lilies and roses.
My love, there isn't a way in this world

a feather on a stone will make anything lighter.
And I know, sadness

has dressed me and trumpeted on.
Each time, I wish I were a beginner, again

at my own grief. Skill–less and accidental.
To know nothing, and live.

We brought a small plant back home
from your father's garden, on our last visit.

When you stand there, hovering over it
as if to make another leaf grow,

I remember, you, too, grew in that garden.
When you dress me,

because I can't, you are life,
dressing me.

Waiting within the Idiom

—After Lousie Glück

George has gone to get some soil.
Didn't I sit on a shovel? Wasn't I waiting?

Isn't that just that?
The umbrella upward?

Twice my father said, "there isn't much to harvest."
Each year he must have pressed from the trees.

Where is my sycamore? How blue is it now?
The horses, orchard–legged across the landfills, trying again—

rain for rain, rain atop its shade. Was that my disappearance?
Local to the room existing for this door?

Isn't that just it?
The umbrella, stepping into its required shape?

Could it not have been more dermal;
the geese shot mid–air and still blue, the sycamore.

Wasn't there a cell for auction?
Wasn't there a bid of joy? Did it think I was insufferable?

Aren't I so present
in my past,
aren't I at least sowing seeds somewhere!

I forgot my hat again. Left
it on his chin. Now, the napes

of my ears are wetting. I hear—yes, I can hear
death's wagons being pulled over a root.

Ekphrastic: Essay for Two Photographs of a Fishbowl 2020, then 2025

"You gotta ask yourself one question. 'Do I feel lucky?' Well, do ya? Punks!" —Jim Carrey, The Mask

The ear away from the other—

it was high time you held me, same as skylarks flutter from their song.

If I am honest, that is what it has been like to grieve—the song of a modest lark. Thievish, predictable. To shamble through its versatile repertoire. To have a whim heave me toward a piano, to play its song by ear. There were times I struggled with the codependency of memory and realm; my husband and I made fish when you went, I saw a heron when you left in a salt–green sky. It moved like a tunnel—I heard life and the moving back towards it. I'd like to invite you to dinner sometime— commonplace things.

Based on your silence, I believe you are well. What to say into this silence, that isn't arrogant? Your left lobe, somewhere in Santa Monica. The right, still as a tassel is before the corn. The clutch is easy, the silk a dress, and all correspondence well–animated.

We're in the car—Garry Moore on. The time, still on daylight savings. At home, a monstera is growing. Left the apartment by nine. Dreamt things all day. Dreamt I was a robin. The blood so close to my throat, like I had known true tenderness.

Last evening, my husband spilled darjeeling onto the table cloth, and later when I hurried errands alone in my green Polo, I saw a red horse in the mist, like he had painted wind and waited for me to go there. Ben, with this band around my finger, I never knew *where* to go.

That long summer I closed my eyes and no one came looking—if you'd been there, you'd have seen it: You could pluck my heart from the linden. I kept climbing hilltops in worry that my joy might mitigate. I'd beg my husband: "Let me love you in advance!" If water itself is not wet, what does that say about this errand of life?

To have been loved by a goldfish once—both, rose and stone around the belt—and not have it remember a thousand times. To pick each other from each other.

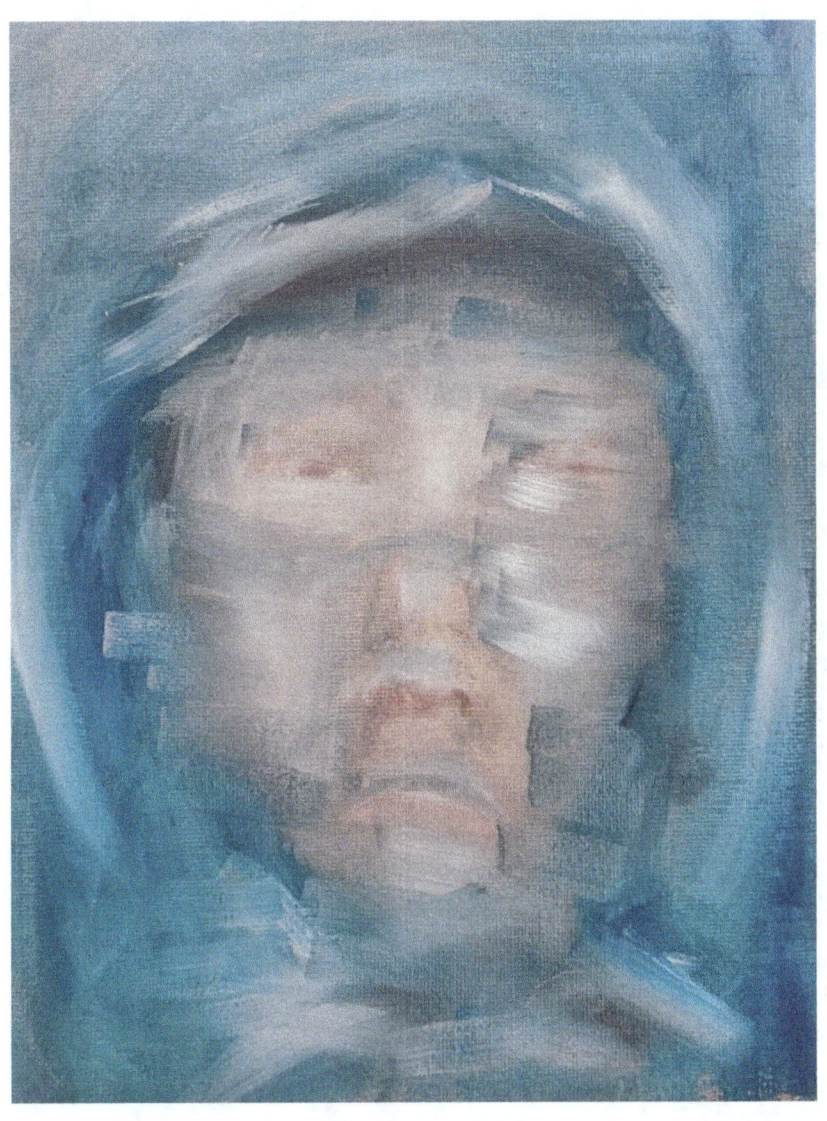

There have been green meadows in the driver's seat, for two countries; these days, the air is like a wet palm around me, the cowlick of my husband's elbow—a mountain's drooping eyelid. It's where I walk to sleep, it's where I walk to wake—legless, listless. Did you walk Kaiser Wilhelms Platz where evergreens had shed their needles, their cone–

syringes and kept the belt and—did you wear one and remember there are 3,000 lakes in Berlin but you only saw canoes on them? Saw your mother, midnight in a bullseye, sewing brailers. Last week, empty as a house cat, I watched through the window as you cried.

Every season I have ached, I have ached for stone age, ash and extinction. Did you see the snowflakes fall like comets? A bit of an overkill. Did you rub a flake against a flake like two stones together and discover fire is only you, searching a green river for your wife's lost copper earring? In January, before the evening's snowfall, the leaves, out in the garden, were still pumpernickel. Late noon's bluebirds chirped across the brittle light and I thought: it's spring!—What to do with my life now?

This missing is a remnant of life. If you were here, you'd see it: If life were a bird, instead of water, I'd think of it, come December; lay myself at the most southern corner of the beds of every motel. I'd wish it well. *Bruise a knee, break a neck.*

Back home, my husband's face is like a full puzzle. Then sings the same bird. Then, I lose my eyesight to the song. Back there, behind his head, I mouth out a tree carrying red like a toolkit for surrender. My husband keeps bumping his feet below the bench, in blue socks. White horses pull their fast cars through the streets; did you ever try to ride them and did they turn into a poster when they saw you?—Everyone sees you in this small town; did you want to leave someone clueless like a borderless thrush? Didn't know what to say after you had said it. Until now, our desire to live hasn't made us

capable. Then, the bird sings a riddle. Then, nose falls from nozzle—he comes apart like a tree; newly hurts each September. His face flakes into his hips. "What lake", he says, "to swim in by myself, knowing the hindsight of skin." He's crowned by a bare tree, until I look again and his face is like a full puzzle, framed by naked arms.

While you are as you are, and are elsewhere, I cannot articulate what time it is; if your life will allow it—unlike egg whites—I'll not be a ghost, only visible in the heat of moments (of which I have so many, to pirate my little life and leave me in a nutshell).

My husband saw another heron, watched it snap a fish. I wonder if it wondered about life the way that I do. He took a picture and mailed it to his dad. Anyhow, I've by now developed a fear of my own words, so let me gaze at you, in friendship.

I am a lousy writer for two reasons: you're flyin'—everything else is fantastical.

Burning Again

In this basil
I am Judas—
don't mean to wake you
when I talk about you,
carsick by your side.
Last year, a single year. While night, while
my husband worried all for nothing,
you were there and drove
that winter—rigid, escalating to a streak.
Parked it beneath my horse–
print scarf
and their unfixed postures,
none of whom were just yet grief.
None I recognized
as manic. I bathed
in those days like a thrush in marbles.
Could not walk
up the stairs like that, recall the room
that had the basil, or where I'd left
what you would bring me, anyway—Storch
of Sadness. You occur to me like a clave
does to a clave. Is this question, or desire:
what heart will lisp through my hands—
whose face between these night–loose
thirds? Fake, but with such true intention.
Isn't that enough?
You have spooned me like a pear
in spring, haven't you?—you have! If I had an ear
like a magpie in the mist
of my husband's mouth, I'd tell this London
artist that no one, up to this hour,
from the moment he had sketched me,

had called
me Jonah, Giona, or Jojo, when
it *is*, in fact, late, I am weary—August is over
and looking for me, all that dead
bread in the toaster is burning again.

Worry Barn

Slowly to my courage,
I climb the duckboards
like a deer into a late October
tree. Or a hand across the black
of an electric piano. Slouch
myself over a shriveled pint.
Honey, the birds are building barns.
Honey, if I had nothing else,
I'd eat the grain from the paper
of the first year of our marriage.
I am always elsewhere when you call,
moving there, airy supplement for
airy supplement—I am cableless.
Walletless by the riverbank across you,
empty socks beneath the bed, and
I cannot what I cannot.
What if I did? Bring you coffee
tomorrow and all of our—
what if all of our
hydrangeas turned blue?

The Miner

When the men walked back down
the mountains, to see
what they had climbed—

axe, carabiners and helmet
still in their arms, the wagons
and rails sat still in the trees.

When the first man held a match
to the coal–seam
of his late wife's

clothes, was it her body
I am keeping warm,
with every poem,

born beneath a mountain?

Night Errands

Across the moon–whitened street,
through bill–lit windows

like through headless
tambourines, I watch the night run

errands; scat down its cleaning
crews—cloth and karaoke.

The Alps turn downward, walk
toward me like nurses

with a belt. Broad shouldered
and head–cut they come.

If ever there was room,

it would be January
before the holly

by the window, on which I'd hang both
my ears, by unused floss and earring.

I'd only ever sit there, beheaded,
at this table,

woolen like the rod
I'd dream our husbands

holding at the docks. Holding
it, how Latin leaves the mouth

with grief. Quiet for the submarines'—the hips'
"silentium"; holding count the silent minute

in a dead language. I could prove nothing
morbid. Meanwhile, another night
in your direction

and my unskilled day as a half–
ridden dark—What's to happen when

the Rockies ring at your door?
How will I reach you then?

Standing in the Past, Moving Forward

Sometimes, the shadow looks
across the room,
says, "I come from light, I must
lay against the grain
of your armhair."
And so, instead
of "I miss you"
I say: "I look forward
to seeing you."
Instead of "I'm thirsty",
I say, "I look forward
to drinking."
I remember you fully,
and know you only half—
standing in the past,
moving:
the body in line with the head,
moving.
It is this, if not another.

Mother Life

Dayflies on
the avocados, beneath
the grocery store roses.

Sometimes, I buy lemons
and let them rot.

Sometimes, mother
brings them home

from Spain,
or elsewhere—

they seem to last
a lifetime.

Wehmutslachen

I eat a sample
of the cantaloupe
on Seinfeld's kitchenette,

when he is looking
directly at me,
and start to laugh.

About your Love, the Cloak

At night, I take it off.
At night I take bread and chisel.
At night I make salt.
At night I fill the ampersand of your gut.
At night, when your heart huffs
my head will send you its skull.
At night I give you a shoelace of breath
and a cape of love.

In October, or Sooner Than

I will need a different shirt.

It was tactless
to have given you mine—of grief,
worn and warm of myself.

To keep
the cloth I'd cut
from it.

It is hot in this cabin of
mystics.

Few of the days I've had to live,
the heart—it had

felt more like a fan
on the ceiling,

than a propeller on the plane.
And what's there?

What's ever there
to surrender?

Lake Turnover

to R.

What is tomorrow
for you? I always have

to calculate. Is it the afternoon
when my coat is wet, twice,

with dog–walk and errand?
Hung over the black rack like
a cheek, to dry over a wet night.

And isn't it such an inconvenience—
to the camel *and* the carpet—
for it to rain through either nostril.

I wake up
        with mist between my arms—

you must be swimming,
        still—some lake

that hasn't turned, yet.
I don't trust time
        does much difference. I turn

and turn; my obsession   and apathy mingle.
        What do you make of that vigour,
                        that I cannot?

Ring–a–ding—I am sounding you the fog bells,
if you cannot see the mother for the milk.

If you cannot see you,
tomorrow—

    I'll see you,
    tomorrow
        —N.

Perpetual Motion

"Sein Mütchen an jemandem kühlen"
— meaning: to cool/let out one's anger on someone, "Mütchen"
diminutive of "Mut", transl.: "courage"

It is noon, when I begin

watching a wildhorse shamble, having just one sandwich and a
metronome—this had been a long year, and I'd only lived to grow
out of it. I am late to the port and in a hurry to love my husband,
perpetually.

I dream I am

one of the women in the herbs
of second–hand clothes, on market–days, from where we drove
along the motorway with hysteric windscreen wipers. Scurried
through security and ran towards the gate with open belts—I once
sang an unfinished song at a pub, and it felt somewhat like it.

The crows had never sunk

on the ice, atop this roof—but I sunk instead, below my own eyes
like their crumb.

Had I not let my hair down, how would he find me? Here with the
lark, I do what needs doing. Here, I do my groundwork of looking
up above. We sit in the airport café, and my husband wears his
glasses. Wears his hair, chestnut like noon. He says, "Einstein must
at least have been related to a pilot."

His shoe—a cajon.

Dore mi—I'm nowhere near dying. Doremifasolatido—nowhere
near.

It's die–cut like that wall,

just molecular like the dream
of that lilac shin,

the young foot that waltzes in and out of sight—aiming to laze
down in the hammock of a furrow, waiting. It is noon,

when on this leather of a dead horse (like a winter I return to), I
write from this Ottawa of mine;

I cooled my mettlelet
on you, far summer day—of your bread
no dog will eat.

Had I not cut the grass, it would be greenest, here.

Had I not been an angel

in the snow, I wouldn't be able to see it, at all.

Bon Voyage, Cosmonaut

Once, my brother hovered with his hand above
your old–dog–tumour. A sphere that, that next Tuesday,

I saw, stood sideways–looking down your chest, as you lay
in your space and suit. Saw an earthlet that was once an earth—

where I had habitat. Where I had shot
my shovel of grief

into its summit. Saw myself,
shrunk to bit and bob. They've put a pin in this haystack,

I am a sleepless beauty. I might spew
my medicine into the snow, once it does—

as it does not seem it will—snow. Nevertheless,
I am allowed on walks and errands and calls. I do my due

to sleep the night, although the current proves
incapable and harmless to the mind.

I might try and dip my toes into the fountain's basin,
tenderly as mist. I have merit for a miracle—often wonder who does
not—

often wonder who will stand beneath a breaking
sky and shout "how weak!"

Don't you miss me, despite? If I walk the fountain, I'll be sure
to tell you. I'll make sure to let you know; I healed the storm.

In this Clock, the Linden

piss from their hearts.

My soul's wet on the bed, mouth like a horse about to neigh.

It does not seem I had a hand

in June—gin, more gin, and no strategy to walk

with any foresight—foresight that's pottered out of hindsight—

when the numbers disappear and leave

no ghost, that is what haunts me.

Somewhere deep ground during the storm

I imagine my feet will be

somewhat like the linden's,

doing this kind of pottery—shame, we will not see

them for our bellies of rock and

Olanzapine. Never knew what to do with this anger

until it was all I was—until I had to keep it.

Now, I seem to remember, its monopoly—

just now, the apex of my ears had cramped,

when it is five to one,

and my good elbows are stacked at six

like some kind of elephant.

The Bird that Flew a Line

If
beneath my tree
it is

autumn, and ability
falls off the body
twice; relentless

and monumental,
could you name
the bird that nudges

into my crown? Sad
sad, circular information—
If

you are law,
then this is
my anarchy;

the rake of lid—
the cloth it is,
until the crumb.

This Tadpole Winter

And the geese and their genetic mercury.
And the things that happen behind its back.
And the cool alarm, not cool enough.
And the individual worry,
and the words that cleaned none.
And how astute, while it.
How warm, this trouble–child.
And my generic route
and the adenine and thymine,
and the formation in which they fly.
And the velcro on their flake.
And the bristle on the load.
And the complement of a season to my sadness.
And the trill in the mild.

The Rain in His Beard

While some of you are making dinner, my entire life
I've moved from trough into rain—from lovedness
to love. The rain in his beard. I'll mark my calendar,

once not. Do that for so many things now. That even a tear might
have bristles.

I'd be like a fox in heather, there
at a funeral—did I have thoughts
on the ferry?—we might as well be honest. I am

urged here, by urges, or perhaps, the lack of it all. Back in August, I
sat

in an office, with my embezzled grief, my inapplicable joy—
on a whim, more like, and had them put my name on a list.
It's January now, and how overdue the volta. (This poem

didn't come to me, I hunted it!) I am lying in and to, as I was at times
to you

(complaining mostly about banal things), in my bed—
we might as well be honest—showered and shaved.
Lying here, beside a key–

lock window, closed curtains like a mortician's yellow accordion,

equipped with these hands. My enamel, by now
a fox's tail. Sleep is hard to regulate—hard to keep hygienic.
I keep missing my turn at Uno. Stillness has a retarded start—
but he kisses me when it comes through the gut. Insanity has its
agents—the mind talks, still

and always. Hums through the nostril, and I cannot give it a coat—
from the trough, again, into the rain, again—I move
from joy into madness. From craft into compulsion.

I should leave it to
its zigzagging. The thoughts to do their work
and once night, they shall go

home to their widows and wives in this body,
and I will lie in bed, a breath

without soil. My griefs and my euphorias share a degree, as
Fahrenheit and Celsius.
What I had anticipated as joy, turned out to be a fraud,
more often than not—I move, move from it into madness—unless,
unless he's had

his hand in it. Good, god!—The resemblance—of us beneath that
sheer umbrella, New Year's Day,

and the phantom catfish in the zoo. Here
is what I think of God: to study himself, he must've created. I might
be his cure.
My heart seems a paradise for these finities. Finities. In the motel
car park

on Christmas Eve, where we'd gone because everything in town was
shut on Christmas Eve—

me, weary and fearing my worst, had a doubt sitting under
my tongue like lorazepam. I'm saying this lovingly: isn't it easier to
converse
in such a way to have someone else speak for you? "I miss you. I
want to be okay.

It's as plain as it should be simple; as for my death, I want to look at it, living."

Anti–Ode to Momentum

To swarm like you do,
into a staircase
of red–riding robins,

beneath which 7 children sit
with their same baskets,
until October's ribbon's flooded

and washed into my hair—
dry, skinny and swinging, swinging.
Good nights, I search the jersey

for tag and aspiration. Christen
their yippee–dee–doo until dissolved.
Did you, as a child, or ever, wear

your clothes backward
and pray, as if
retreating into the gods?

Robbed, I Give to You

                Robbed,
                I give to you
this goat.

                It is both, surrender and essay

                in one,

                of which to sew
                leather 'round our corduroy couch.
On which

                you drive night for night—

                both, *Seinfeld* and console heatless—drive toward my indication,

                that, too, is soluble now,
                like you say about the hybrids on the highway. Soluble beneath
the bucket's

                flooring, beneath the dripping ceiling. My failure

                to be well

                isn't your failure—I am missing the snow. How it blackens
                the paint like a horse's eye, calming—while still black, the willow,
pacing

                like broom and dust, it seems

                evident that

                I would move
                without particular destination—
I give

                these prophets their mountains.

You need

a long breath
for this kind of life.

I give

these prophets their mountains.

Autumn's Quiet Prescription of Falling

"To be, or not to be" —*William Shakespeare*

I've forgotten the question
I meant to ask here. To be
rustling now, up
with energy—
I feel so distant
to my suffering,
while its eye
is in my socket,
and mine
is in its lamp. How
I'll hold it, still,
my t–zone. Shave
a beard, not to be
around us.

Portrait of Grief as an Orphan

to Mark C.

Bed–strung this trimester, this is my joyest sad—
Have this poem, have it. Terrible

as it may be, I do not know
enough to dream of going elsewhere—

I fear, if it is good
I'd take my 7th foot
off gas and throttle.

I fear my evil martyrs
are not ready.

But what a bear–
ing

the heart has gone
in.

I ask the monarch:
"what about
your cubs?

They've got to eat!"
And so they do
as much as I—

My long–let mouth
across this long–let leaf.

Have you been so well

within your grief

that you've let your beard
grow 'round it? I've grown accustomed

to my fuzzy legs, where's the damn
to give about what's there to carry,

as small as residual,
not at all opportune.

Isn't the maple, too, only barking
at its red–lot of wings?

One day autumn, we won't have desire
for a blindfold—one day spring

the cocoon will be more
womb than coffin.

I hope what grief has eaten
will morph into a monarch.

I hope you write to me,
from pine oak forests in October,

somewhere southamerica,
where your lungs had not been, yet—

where the monarchs migrate
in September, and then return

to you, brushing back
the snow in March.

Near Calgary, Nearly

a beard around us.

Do you sometimes think

in summer's green,

of my feet

as purple scabious?

Let me,

and weep.

I fell into life

like one falls out of love.

There's always the other

who does the better loving—

which is how the heart

carries me, now

that I've put it down

on the page.

My toes, mind you,

are purple, still.

I Pray this Poem Won't Outlive Me

This is my canister:

being able to explain my trouble.

When I rang

the doorbell that night

as if rowing my maiden

name forward into yours

in that small canoe

of the doorbell panel, blue

roses sewn from toe

to knee, the nude

thighs as if a to back–

comb March's snow,

the roof

you stood under with your jaw

dropped like a chord

into my hat,

was there a bridge that I would think

I'd cross beneath

like sunlight or water?

Instead, I stood out and in

like water that climbs the dam

as snow—each motion, un–motioned.

When'll have gone out

for bits and bobs

and groceries, I will have

danced like that

on the other side

of it—what perfect

tense prophecy is.

Little Bird

Inconsequential, it seems—
the poem. All that shilly–shally
Whenever evening,
whenever sore of sight.
And I've sat in this correspondence
like a kalashnikov in a faux hand.

'round my fat, my residue
of good—my resilience.
Just the how I do, never
once how I do *it*, or

where I've lost
my grace in the meantime.
I curl up
like an angry little bird

and fall into the snow like a deer.
While you are as you are, and are otherwising me,
I'll be quiet,
until it sounds funny,
and then I'll *laugh–and–laugh–and–laugh.*

Monologue into a Cello after Seeing my Figure in Moving Water

—Poem with a question, posed by Joaquín Baldwin, artist of the Spooning Centaur Meme

At the little nobs, I'd cut
the rose stalks in a downward motion.
Dipped the spears in honey and stuck
them into small potatoes, covered each in cellophane
and soil, and added water for good measure.

I waited all summer, but nothing.
These days, the hands into which I've wept, only take
the sheets out the dryer and run
along their edges—a quality check of some sort.
It started when my hands themselves were still damp,

rolling up and down your shirts to collect
what love the dog had left there.
Back then, I could steam your work clothes
in my grief. Darling, I don't think we took
the time to appreciate that yet another stone

had reached its mile. Been carrying theses stones
in my pockets for quite some time now—
always careful not to lie too low, or to jump too high.
To never touch a joy I couldn't dismantle—I am
what road I am. I walk what road I walk with you.

I am a centaur of desire and dust,
still in cellophane—now you're up again
wondering with what part of me I'll spoon you,

still waiting for me to grow a wing
on the tip of someone's absence,

straggle your beard 'round cold memory—
but I have discovered a smile that does not hide
agony. George, I saw it from the shore today.
And boy, do I have a big nose! I could tell the white horses
had a hard time coming down it.

I tossed the stones into the water like sugar cubes,
remembered my horseback riding lessons
and almost falling out of the saddle down slope like that.
When you look at me, you make a sound like *huff*.
Like instead I am one

of the rose–grafts
in my mother's garden,
early in June, or July—
how often has wonder been made
by those who wonder.

Driving Back from Torrevieja, I had Grieved My State of Mind

The moon had grown over the Highstreet.
I hummed. I hung
my arms out the window,

luring myself into the rocks.
We got out. Walked
with lilies on our heads—

the hilltop on the cape
like a dark thumb, pressed into the clouds.
Yellow dust dangling everywhere.

Notes on Previous Publication

Serif Serif
was named a finalist of the Peatsmoke Summer Poetry Contest in 2023

To George, in the Distance
was published in Eunoia Review in October 2023

The Ungiving
was published in ONE ART in December 2023

Worry Barn & Burning Again
were published in The Poetry Society of New York, in 2024

In October, or Sooner Than
was published in San Pedro River Review's spring issue in 2024.

Night Errands
was published in Tupelo Quarterly in spring 2024 as finalist of the TQ32 Poetry Open.

The poems *Moss Study* and *Basin–Cut* were written as part of a letter series in collaboration with Rachael Moorthy. *Lake Turnover* was written as the latest letter in the series.

Thanks

Thank you to my *husband* and forever love, for being my steady rock throughout the stories behind these poems. You make me laugh though the downpour, make me stronger, smarter. I'd turn thirty in your arms all over again, just to show you how beautiful you are.

Thank you to my Editor, *Emily Perkovich,* for taking on this manuscript and attaching wings to it. I am happy it has found a home with you at *Querencia Press,* and is in such good, caring hands.

Thank you to *Susan L. Leary, Rachael Moorthy,* and *Katy Luxem* for your generous words on *Salamander Morning.* You have been an inspiration to me and my writing. To have you reflect so warmly on my work means the world to me.

www.ingramcontent.com/pod-product-compliance
Lightning Source LLC
Chambersburg PA
CBHW071218120626
46546CB00006B/2615